Steck-Vaughn

BRIDGES TO READING COMPREHENSION

Level A/B

ACKNOWLEDGMENTS

EXECUTIVE EDITOR: Diane Sharpe
PROJECT EDITOR: Anne Souby
DESIGN MANAGER: Donna Brawley
PHOTO EDITOR: Margie Foster
PRODUCT DEVELOPMENT: Curriculum Concepts

ILLUSTRATION CREDITS: Unit 1 Lyle Miller: pp.33-37, 39-41; Unit 2 Jan Naimo Jones: pp.75-79, 81-83; Unit 3 Dennis Davidson: pp.88-89; Ellen Joy Sasaki: pp.97-101, 103-104; Michael McDermott: pp.116-121, 123-125.

PHOTO CREDITS: Unit 1 p.4 (kids) © Tony Freeman/PhotoEdit, (zebras) © S.J. Krasemann/Peter Arnold, Inc.; p.5 (elephant) © John Callahan/Tony Stone Images, (dog) © Tim Davis/Photo Researchers, (wolf) © John M. Burnley/Photo Researchers, (cat) © David Young-Wolff/PhotoEdit; p.6 © Tom Leeson/Photo Researchers; p.7 © Jeff Lepore/Photo Researchers; p.8 © Tim Davis/Photo Researchers; p.9 Courtesy Department of Library Services-American Museum of Natural History; p.10 © Jeff Lepore/Photo Researchers; p.11 (a) © John M. Burnley/Photo Researchers, (b, d-f, h-l) © Cooke Photographics, (c) © Michael & Barbara Reed/Animals Animals; p.12 Courtesy Department of Library Services-American Museum of Natural History; p.13 © John M. Burnley/Photo Researchers; p.14 © Tim Davis/Photo Researchers; p.15 © Lawrence Migdale/Photo Researchers; p.16 © Guy Gillette/Photo Researchers; p.17 © Norm Thomas/Photo Researchers; p.18 © George Holton/Photo Researchers; p.19 © Lawrence Migdale/Photo Researchers; p.20 (a-g, i-l) © Cooke Photographics; p.21 © Norm Thomas/Photo Researchers; p.22 © Guy Gillette/Photo Researchers; pp.24-28, 30 © Margaret Miller/Photo Researchers; p.29 © Cooke Photographics; p.31 (cat) © Rhoda Sidney/PhotoEdit, (dog) © Myrleen Ferguson/PhotoEdit, (horse) © Alan D. Carey/Photo Researchers; p.32 © Margaret Miller/Photo Researchers; p.38 © Cooke Photographics; Unit 2 p.42 (soccer) © Tony Freeman/PhotoEdit, (marbles) © Tony Freeman/PhotoEdit; p.43 (baseball) © Richard Hutchings/PhotoEdit, (basketball) © Tony Freeman/PhotoEdit, (jump rope) Suzanne Szasz/Photo Researchers; p.44 © Paul Conklin/Monkmeyer Press Photo Service; p.45 © Stephen Ogilvy; p.46 © Spencer Grant/Monkmeyer Press Photo Service; p.47 © Stephen Ogilvy; p.48 © Bill Backmann/PhotoEdit; p.49 © Richard Hutchings/PhotoEdit; p.50 (soccer) © Tony Freeman/PhotoEdit, (a, c-d, f-h) © Cooke Photographics, (c) © David Omer, (e) © Zig Leszczynski/Animals Animals; p.51 ©Suzanne Szasz/Photo Researchers; p.52 © Stephen Ogilvy; p.53 © Spencer Grant/Monkmeyer Press Photo Service; p.54 © Charles Gupton/Tony Stone Images; p.55 © Harvey Lloyd/The Stock Market; p.56 © Stephen Ogilvy; p.57 © Pamela Johnson Meyer/Photo Researchers; p.58 © Stephen McBrady/PhotoEdit; p.59 © Harvey Lloyd/The Stock Market; p.60 © Cooke Photographics; p.61 © Harvey Lloyd/The Stock Market; p.63 © Stephen McBrady/PhotoEdit; pp.64-69, 71-72 Courtesy Woody Pumphrey; p.70 (a,e) © Cooke Photographics, (b-c, f-h) © David Omer, (d) © Joseph Schuyler/Stock Boston; p.74 © Culver Pictures; p.80 (a) © David Omer, (b, e-h) © Cooke Photographics, (c) © David Omer, (d) © Bill Records; Unit 3 p.84 (night sky) © Tony Freeman/PhotoEdit, (skyline) © Joseph Foldes/Monkmeyer Press Photo Service; p.85 (tree) © Peter Arnold, (moon) © Lick Observatory; p.86 © Kitt Peak/SPL/Photo Researchers; p.87 © John Sanford/SPL/Photo Researchers; p.90 © Jerry Schad/Photo Researchers; p.91 © Kitt Peak/SPL/Photo Researchers; p.92 (a-c, e-f) © David Omer, (d) © Animals Animals; p.93 © Peter Arnold; p.94 © John Sanford/SPL/Photo Researchers; p.95 © Jerry Schad/Photo Researchers; p.96 © 1960 Turner Entertainment Co. All Rights Reserved; p.102 (a-b, d-e) © David Omer, (c) © John I. Pointier/Animals Animals, (f) © Dennis MacDonald/Unicorn; p.106 © NASA; p.107 © Galen Rowell/Peter Arnold, Inc.; p.111 © NASA; p.112 (a) © David Omer, (b-d, f) © Cooke Photographics, (e) © Animals Animals; p.113 © Galen Rowell/Peter Arnold, Inc.; p.122 (a-c, e) © David Omer, (d) Stephen Dalton/Animals Animals, (f) © George Bellerose/Stock Boston.

Grateful acknowledgment is made for permission to reprint copyrighted material as follows:
Working Dogs by Max Marquardt. Copyright © 1989 American Teacher Publications.

ISBN 0-8114-5741-9

Copyright © 1995 Steck-Vaughn Company.

All rights reserved. No part of the material protected by this copyright may be reproduced or utilized in any form or by any means, electronic or mechanical, including photocopying, recording, or by any information storage and retrieval system, without permission in writing from the copyright owner. Requests for permission to make copies of any part of the work should be mailed to Copyright Permissions, Steck-Vaughn Company, P.O. Box 26015, Austin, Texas 78755.

Printed in the United States of America.

3 4 5 6 7 8 9 0   BP   00 99 98 97 96

Contents

UNIT 1 — Animal Friends

- Lesson 1 • Save the Animals 6
- Lesson 2 • Working Dogs 15
- Lesson 3 • Growing Up 24
- Lesson 4 • Funny Monkey 33

UNIT 2 — Games Kids Play

- Lesson 5 • Street Games 44
- Lesson 6 • Games Around the World 54
- Lesson 7 • The Jump Rope Kids 64
- Lesson 8 • A New Old Game 74

UNIT 3 — The Sky Above Us

- Lesson 9 • All About Stars 86
- Lesson 10 • Traveling Through Time 96
- Lesson 11 • The Changing Moon 106
- Lesson 12 • A Summer to Remember 116

My Word List 126

UNIT

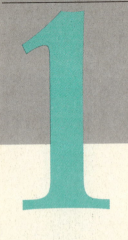

Animal Friends

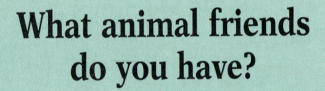

What animal friends do you have?

Animals are an important part of life on Earth. Some animals are wild. Some animals are pets. We think of many animals as friends. Some animals can help people. But some animals need people to help them.

As you read this unit, you will learn more about animals. You will find out what good friends they can be!

What Do You Already Know?

Look at these animals. Which ones are wild? Which ones are pets? How do you know? Write two words that tell how each animal looks.

_____   _____

_____   _____

_____   _____

_____   _____

What Do You Want to Find Out?

You will read stories about different animals in this unit. What do you want to find out about animals? Write two questions on the lines. You may find the answers as you read.

_____

_____

_____

_____

Lesson 1

GETTING READY TO READ

The first story you will read is "Save the Animals." Do you know that some animals need our help? How do you think people can help save wild animals?

What Do You Think You Will Learn?

Look at pages 7 through 9. Look at the pictures. What do you think you will learn in the story? Draw a line under the sentence that tells what you think.

I will learn about dogs and cats.

I will learn about wild animals that are in danger.

SAVE THE ANIMALS

People share the world with many kinds of animals. Today, many of these animals are in danger. You'll learn about a few of these animals in this story. You will also learn what you can do to help them.

Wolves on Vancouver Island in Canada are in danger. Hunters trap them. Then they sell the fur. Now there are not many of these wolves left. Many people are working hard to save these wolves. They want to stop the hunting now.

These wolves live together in small packs.

Elephants were in danger in East Africa. Elephants need much land to live on. People need that land, too. This caused problems.

People moved onto the land where elephants lived. People cleared the land to build houses. They cleared away the grass and plants that elephants need for food. The elephants began to die.

Elephants were also in danger from hunters. They would kill elephants for their long, white tusks. Elephant tusks were sold for very much money.

Hunters used to kill elephants for their white tusks.

Some people got angry. They wanted to help the elephants. These people worked hard. They set up special parks for the elephants to live in. It is against the law to hunt in these parks. Today people visit from all over the world. They like watching the elephants and other animals.

The blue whale is a huge animal. It is the biggest animal in the world. People hunt the whales for their meat. Whales are also hunted for their oil. Every year, there are fewer blue whales. Today, many people are trying to stop the hunting. They are trying to save the blue whale.

The blue whale is 100 feet long and weighs more than 150 tons.

Many people work hard to save the animals. More can be done. How can you help? Write to a zoo. Find out what the people there do. Or join a wildlife club. Most zoos and clubs help save animals in danger. You can help, too!

Lesson 1

AFTER READING

What Did You Learn?

You have read "Save the Animals" for the first time. What did you want to find out? Look on page 6 to help you remember. Did you learn anything that you didn't know before? Write on the lines below. You can look back at the story to help you.

_____

_____

_____

Check Your Understanding

Darken the circle next to the word that best completes each sentence.

1. All over the world _____ are in danger.
    - Ⓐ people
    - Ⓑ animals
    - Ⓒ buildings

2. Hunters kill wolves for their _____.
    - Ⓐ fur
    - Ⓑ tails
    - Ⓒ teeth

3. Many people are working hard to _____ wild animals.
    - Ⓐ hunt
    - Ⓑ chase
    - Ⓒ save

4. Today elephants live in special _____.
    - Ⓐ countries
    - Ⓑ parks
    - Ⓒ barns

Lesson 1

Word Analysis — Initial Consonants

Say each picture name. Write the letter that stands for each beginning sound.

1. ___olf
2. ___op
3. ___at
4. ___ock
5. ___ish
6. ___ero
7. ___at
8. ___ot
9. ___og
10. ___ake
11. ___ase
12. ___one

Look back in the story. Find two words that have the same **beginning** sound you hear in **fish**. Say the words to yourself. Write the words here.

_____   _____

11

Lesson 1

Vocabulary — Pictures as Context Clues

Pictures can help you understand what a word means. Read this sentence from the story.

The blue whale is a huge animal.

Look at the word huge. Then look at the picture of the whale. What can you tell about the whale? The whale is very big. Huge means "very big."

Read each sentence from the story. Then look at the picture on the page. Circle the word or words that tell what the word in dark print means.

1. These wolves live together in small **packs**. (page 7)

    houses   groups   places

2. Hunters used to kill elephants for their white **tusks**. (page 8)

    long teeth   ears   skins

Words That Were New to You

Choose other words from the story that were new to you. Use a dictionary to check the meanings. Add the words and their meanings to your word list on page 126.

Lesson 1

REREADING

Cause and Effect

Sometimes one thing makes another happen. What happens is called the **effect**. Why it happens is called the **cause**. Read these sentences from "Save the Animals."

> Wolves on Vancouver Island in Canada are in danger. Hunters trap them.

In these sentences, hunters trap them is the cause. The effect is that the wolves are in danger.

Read "Save the Animals" again. Look for other causes and effects. Ask yourself, "What happened?" and "Why did it happen?" It will help you to understand the story better. It will also help you to understand what will happen next.

After you reread the story, fill in this chart. Look back at the story to help you.

Cause (Why did it happen?)	Effect (What happened?)
Hunters trap wolves.	Wolves are in danger.
People cleared away the grass and plants that elephants need for food.	
People hunt blue whales for their meat and oil.	

13

Lesson 1

THINK and WRITE

Think about what you have learned. Choose one of these activities to complete.

1. Find out how you can help wild animals, too. What would you like to learn about saving animals? Make a list of questions. Then write a letter to

    World Wildlife Fund, Inc.
    1250 24th Street NW, Suite 400
    Washington, D.C. 20037

2. Suppose you were visiting a wild animal park in Africa. Which animals would you like to see? Why? Tell about it.

3. Show one way people can help wild animals in danger. Draw a picture to show what people can do. Then write a sentence about it.

4. Why do you think it's important to save the animals? Make up a bumper sticker that gives your reason. Draw a picture to go on your bumper sticker.

Lesson 2

GETTING READY TO READ

In this story you will read about working dogs. Working dogs do jobs that help people. What jobs do you think that dogs do?

What Do You Think You Will Learn?

Look at pages 16 through 18. Look at the pictures. What do you think you will learn in the story? Draw a line under the sentence that tells what you think.

I will learn how working dogs help people.

I will learn how working dogs play.

WORKING DOGS

A dog can make a good pet. But there are dogs that are not pets. They are working dogs.

Working dogs can do many jobs. They do many things to help people.

Bonnie is a working dog. She helps Don. Don can't see.

Bonnie and Don go out. Bonnie leads Don. If Bonnie stops, Don stops. If Bonnie goes, Don goes, too.

This man can't see. The dog helps him.

The trainer is teaching this dog to climb the fence.

Rocky is a working dog. He works with the police. He helps stop crime.

Working dogs need to be trained to do jobs. Rocky had to be trained to do police work. This man helped train Rocky to do his job.

Koko is a working dog. She leads a team of working dogs. Koko and the team work in the snow.

These dog teams pull sleds through the snow.

Dog teams pull sleds. They run in the snow. In places with lots of snow, sled dogs help people get from place to place.

People are happy to have working dogs. Working dogs do many jobs. They help people do many things.

From *Working Dogs*, by Max Marquardt

Lesson 2

AFTER READING

What Did You Learn?

You have read "Working Dogs" for the first time. What did you think you would learn? Look back on page 15 to help you remember. Did you learn anything new? Tell about it. Write on the lines below. You can look back at the story to help you.

_____

_____

_____

_____

Check Your Understanding

Darken the circle next to the word that best completes each sentence.

1. Working dogs do jobs to help _____.

    Ⓐ animals   Ⓑ people   Ⓒ pets

2. When Don goes out, Bonnie _____ him.

    Ⓐ leads   Ⓑ follows   Ⓒ drives

3. Rocky helps to stop _____.

    Ⓐ work   Ⓑ crime   Ⓒ play

4. Koko and the team of dogs pull _____ in the snow.

    Ⓐ sleds   Ⓑ horses   Ⓒ cars

Lesson 2

Word Analysis — Final Consonants

Say each picture name. Write the letter that stands for each ending sound.

1. do___
2. be___
3. ga___
4. ja___
5. for___
6. gu___
7. cu___
8. quil___
9. fa___
10. si___
11. ca___
12. nai___

Read these sentences. Circle the words that have the same **ending** sound you hear in bed.

A dog can make a good pet.

Koko and the team work in the snow.

20

Lesson 2

Vocabulary — Inflectional Endings

A verb is a word that shows action. A verb tells what a person, place, or thing does. When you add -s to a verb, the action is happening now. When you add -ed to a verb, the action happened in the past. Read the sentences below.

1. The dog team pulls the sled now.

2. The dog team pulled the sled last night.

The word pull is an action word. It tells what the dog team is doing. In sentence 1, -s is added to pull. Pulls tells what the dog team is doing now. In sentence 2, -ed is added to pull. Pulled tells you what the dog team did in the past.

Read these sentences. Is the action happening now or did it happen in the past? Circle the word that completes each sentence.

1. Rocky _____ with police now.
   works   worked

2. A man _____ Rocky last year.
   trains   trained

3. Rocky _____ stop crime now.
   helps   helped

Words That Were New to You

Choose words from the story that were new to you. Use a dictionary to check the meanings. Add the words and their meanings to your word list on page 126.

21

L e s s o n   2

REREADING

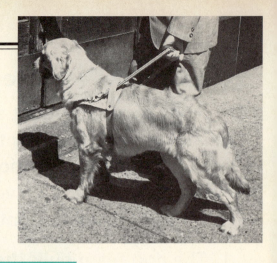

Word Referents

A **noun** is the name of a person, place, or thing. A **pronoun** can stand for a noun in a sentence. Look at these pronouns.

| he | she | they | we | it |

Read these sentences.

> Bonnie is a working dog. She helps Don.

The word *she* is a pronoun. *She* stands for the noun *Bonnie*. Try using *Bonnie* in place of *she*. The sentence still makes sense.

Read these sentences. The words in dark print are pronouns. Circle the noun that the pronoun stands for.

1. Working dogs can do many jobs. **They** do many things to help people.

2. Rocky is a working dog. **He** works with the police.

Read the story again. Look for pronouns and the nouns they stand for. Read page 18. Find one pronoun. Find the noun that the pronoun stands for. Write the sentences on the lines. Circle the noun. Underline the pronoun.

3. _____

_____

Lesson 2

Cause and Effect

The **cause** is why something happens. The **effect** is what happens. Complete this cause and effect chart. Look back at the story to help you.

Cause (Why does it happen?)	Effect (What happens?)
because Bonnie stops	
because Bonnie goes	
because Rocky works with the police	

Think about what you have learned. Then complete one of these activities.

1. What kind of food do you think working dogs need? Make up an ad for a dog food made just for working dogs. Give your dog food a name. Tell how it helps working dogs.

2. Make up a story about a working dog. Then draw pictures to show what happens in your story. Tell your story to a friend.

3. Which kind of working dog would you like to learn more about? Find some information at the library. Write about the dog.

23

Lesson 3

GETTING READY TO READ

In this story you will read about puppies. Puppies are baby dogs. Suppose you had a puppy. What would you do with your puppy?

What Do You Think You Will Learn?

Look at pages 25 through 27. Look at the pictures. What do you think you will learn in the story? Draw a line under the sentence that tells what you think.

I will learn how puppies grow up.

I will learn how big dogs play.

Growing UP

These puppies are one week old. They are very small. The puppies cannot see. They cannot hear yet. The puppies stay near their mother. They sleep near each other to stay warm.

The puppies sleep close together. They keep each other warm.

The puppies do not have any teeth. They cannot chew. They get milk from their mother. The warm milk will help the puppies grow.

The puppies grow. They are four weeks old. Now they can see and hear. The puppies are learning to run around and play together. The puppies are growing up!

The puppies are growing teeth. They can eat soft food. Their mother stays near them. The puppies eat. Then they sleep. Soon the puppies will wake up and eat again. Eating and sleeping help the puppies grow.

The puppies eat soft food from a bowl.

The puppies are playing together.

Look at the puppies now! They are eight weeks old. They do not sleep as much anymore. They can do many things.

They like to play and play.

Rex can roll on his back. Max chases a ball into the playhouse. It rolls under a toy sailboat. Bess hides inside the doghouse. She likes it there. Lucy chews on her toy. She likes to chew on newspapers, too! Her teeth are very sharp. Sam likes to sit on the mat by the mailbox.

The puppies are still growing. One day the puppies will be big dogs. How big do you think they will be?

Lesson 3

After Reading

What Did You Learn?

You have read "Growing Up" for the first time. What did you think you would learn? Look on page 24 to help you remember. Did you learn anything new? Tell about it. Write on the lines below. You can look back at the story to help you.

_____

_____

_____

Check Your Understanding

Darken the circle next to the word that best completes each sentence.

1. Puppies need their mother's _____ to help them grow.

   Ⓐ milk   Ⓑ teeth   Ⓒ toy

2. Puppies cannot _____ when they are one week old.

   Ⓐ hear   Ⓑ eat   Ⓒ sleep

3. Puppies need _____ to help them grow.

   Ⓐ games   Ⓑ toys   Ⓒ sleep

4. Puppies do not have any _____ when they are one week old.

   Ⓐ teeth   Ⓑ ears   Ⓒ eyes

Lesson 3

Word Analysis — Short a and e

Ham has the **short a** vowel sound.

Jet has the **short e** vowel sound.

Say each picture name. Write **a** or **e** if you hear a short vowel sound.

1.
2.
3.
4.
5.
6.
7.
8.

Say each picture name. Circle the story word that has the same vowel sound.

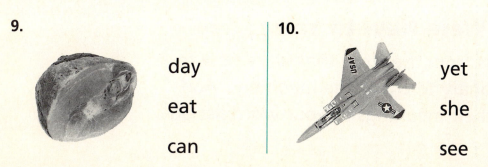

9. day
   eat
   can

10. yet
    she
    see

29

Lesson 3

Vocabulary — Compound Words

Sometimes two small words are put together to make a larger word. The larger word is called a **compound word**. Look at this sentence.

    Bess hides in the doghouse.

Doghouse is a compound word. It is made up of the smaller words **dog** and **house**. The two smaller words may help you find the meaning of the larger word. **Doghouse** means "a house for dogs."

Read these sentences from the story. Circle the compound word in each sentence. Write the two small words that make the compound word.

1. Max chases a ball into the playhouse.

   _____ _____

2. It rolls under a toy sailboat.

   _____ _____

3. She likes to chew on newspapers, too!

   _____ _____

4. Sam likes to sit on the mat by the mailbox.

   _____ _____

Words That Were New to You

Choose words from the story that were new to you. Use a dictionary to check the meanings. Add the words and their meanings to your word list on page 126.

30

Lesson 3

REREADING

Main Idea

Pictures can show one big idea. A big idea is called a **main idea**. Look at the pictures. Read each sentence. Each sentence tells about one picture.

Cats are fun.

Dogs are fun.

Horses are fun.

1. What main idea do all of the pictures show you? Underline the sentence that tells the main idea of all the pictures.

    The girl likes the dog.

    Animals are fun.

    A horse is fast.

Stories have main ideas. Read "Growing Up" again. Underline the main idea of each page.

2. What is the main idea of page 26?

    The puppies are growing up.

    The puppies eat and sleep.

    The puppies have teeth.

3. What is main idea of page 27?

    Rex can roll on his back.

    The puppies can do many things.

    The puppies are eight weeks old.

Lesson 3

Word Referents

Read these sentences. The word in dark print is a pronoun. Circle the noun that the pronoun stands for.

1. These puppies are one week old.

   They are very small.

2. Max loves to play.

   He chases a ball.

3. Bess hides inside the doghouse.

   She likes it there.

4. The puppies eat.

   Then **they** sleep.

Think about what you have learned. Then complete one of these activities.

1. Which of the puppies in the story would you like to have as pet? Tell why.

2. Plan a doghouse. Draw a picture of it. Then tell how you would build it.

3. Suppose you are an eight week old puppy. You are outside for the first time. What do you see? What do you hear? Write about it.

Lesson 4

GETTING READY TO READ

Would you like to have a monkey for a pet? What would you do with this different kind of pet? The story you are going to read is "Funny Monkey." It's a different kind of pet story!

What Do You Think You Will Learn?

Read the title of this story. Then look at pages 34 through 36. What do you see in the pictures? What do you think you will learn in the story? Draw a line under the sentence that tells what you think.

I will learn how Maria gets a pet monkey.

I will learn about Maria's brother.

33

Funny Monkey

Maria wanted a pet. She had always wanted a pet. Maria loved all kinds of animals. She wanted an animal friend of her own. Maria wished she could have a pet to take care of.

Maria's best friend Anna had a very silly dog. He did really goofy things. His name was Buster. Buster had very long legs. He looked very funny when he ran. His legs seemed to go everywhere!

Sometimes Maria and Anna walked Buster to the park. Buster would dance around as soon as he saw the other dogs! That always made Maria laugh. It also made Maria wish even more that she had a pet.

Maria's family lived in a big apartment building. No one there could own a dog. Maria was very sad about that. Her mom got her a fluffy orange kitten. But the kitten made her brother sick.

Then, Maria's father had a surprise for her. He took her to the zoo. A zoo worker told Maria and her father about a special program. It was called "Adopt a Zoo Animal."

Here is how the program worked. First, Maria could pick out the animal that she wanted to adopt. Then, she could give money to the zoo to help care for the animal. Finally, the zoo would send her a picture of that animal.

Maria and her father spent three Saturdays looking at animals. Maria looked at bears and tigers. She looked at snakes and elephants. But the animal Maria liked best was a funny monkey.

The monkey ran around in circles. It clapped its hands. Maria even thought it smiled!

The zoo worker told Maria that the monkey cost $25 to adopt. That was a lot of money! How would she get it? Maybe her friends could help.

Maria talked to her friends. They decided to have a street fair. The children made a poster. It said, "Help us adopt a funny monkey! Come to the Funny Monkey Fair!"

Everyone gave something to sell. Maria sold cookies. Her brother sold lemonade. Anna made picture cards.

At the end of the day, Maria had enough money! She adopted the funny monkey. Four weeks later she got a letter from the zoo. She got a picture, too! What do you think she named the monkey? If you guessed Funny Monkey, you're right!

Lesson 4

AFTER READING

What Did You Learn?

You have read "Funny Monkey" for the first time. What did you think you would find out? Look on page 33 to help you remember. What do you think is different about Maria's pet? Tell what you think. Write on the lines below. You can look back at the story to help you.

_____

_____

_____

Check Your Understanding

Darken the circle next to the word that best completes each sentence.

1. Maria wanted a _____ of her very own.

    Ⓐ pet   Ⓑ book   Ⓒ zoo

2. Maria decided to _____ a zoo animal.

    Ⓐ buy   Ⓑ draw   Ⓒ adopt

3. To raise money, Maria and her friends had a street _____.

    Ⓐ dance   Ⓑ parade   Ⓒ fair

4. Maria adopted a funny _____.

    Ⓐ monkey   Ⓑ lion   Ⓒ elephant

Lesson 4

Word Analysis — Short i, o, and u

Fish has the **short i** vowel sound.

Mop has the **short o** vowel sound.

Rug has the **short u** vowel sound.

Say each picture name. Write **i** or **o** or **u** if you hear a short vowel sound.

Say the word in dark print. Read the sentence. Circle the words in the sentence that have the same short vowel sound as the word in dark print.

mop   Maria's mom got her a kitten.

fish   The kitten made her brother sick.

rug   The funny pet jumped up and down.

38

Lesson 4

Vocabulary — Synonyms

Some words have almost the same meaning. These words are called **synonyms**. The words big and large are synonyms. Read these sentences.

Anna had a very silly dog.
He did goofy things.

The second sentence tells more about the silly dog. He did goofy things. So, goofy and silly have almost the same meaning.

Read each pair of sentences. Look at the word in dark print. Look for a synonym for that word in the other sentence. Write the synonym on the line.

1. Buster made Maria **giggle**. She would laugh at him.

    giggle — _____

2. Maria's mom gave her a **fluffy** kitten. The kitten was soft.

    fluffy — _____

3. A street fair was a **clever** idea. Everyone thought it was a smart thing.

    clever — _____

Words That Were New to You

Choose words from the story that were new to you. Use a dictionary to check the meanings. Add the words and the meanings to your word list on page 126.

Lesson 4

REREADING

Sequence

You do things in order. First, you put on your socks. Then, you put on your shoes. Things in a story happen in order, too.

Sometimes writers use **clue words**. Some clue words to look for are *first*, *then*, *next*, *last*, and *finally*. Read these sentences.

First, Maria wanted a pet. **Then**, she got a cat. **Next**, the cat made her brother sick.

The words in dark print are clue words. They help you understand the order in which things happened.

Read the story again. In what order did these things happen? Write 1, 2, or 3 before each sentence.

1. Here's how the "Adopt an Animal" program works.

    _____ Finally, the zoo sends a picture of your animal.

    _____ Next, give money to the zoo to take care of the animal.

    _____ First, pick an animal.

2. This is what happened in the story.

    _____ Then, Maria and her friends had a street fair.

    _____ First, Maria wanted to get money to adopt a pet.

    _____ Finally, Maria got the money.

Lesson 4

Main Idea

The main idea is the most important idea of a story. Everything else in the story tells more about the main idea. What is the most important idea in "Funny Monkey"? Underline the sentence that tells that idea. Look back at the story to help you.

1. Some apartment buildings will not let people have dogs.

2. Maria's favorite zoo animal is a monkey.

3. Maria adopts a monkey at the zoo.

You have read about Maria's special pet. Choose and complete one of these activities about pets.

1. Learn more about the "Adopt an Animal" programs at different zoos. Think about what you want to find out. Make a list of three questions. Then write to
    American Association of Zoological Parks
      and Aquariums, Oglebay Park
    Wheeling, WV 26003-1698

2. What funny things do you think the monkey does? Tell a funny story about the monkey.

3. Which zoo animal would you like to adopt? Why do you like this animal? Find a fact about this animal. Use a book in your school library to help you. Then tell about the animal.

41

UNIT 2
GAMES KIDS PLAY

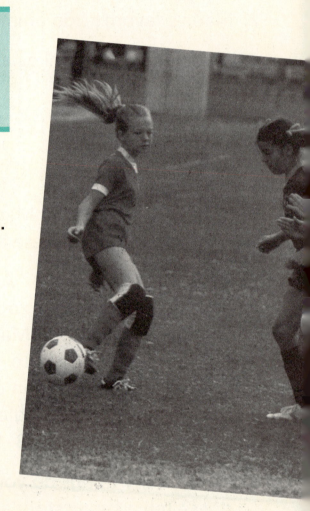

Why do you play games?

Some games are old. Children have played them for years and years. Some games are new. Some games are played by the street, some in a park, and some at home. There are games to play with teams or with a friend. But all the games are alike in one important way. They are all a lot of fun!

What Do You Already Know?

Look at these pictures of different games. Write a sentence that tells what you know about each one.

_____

_____

_____

What Do You Want to Find Out?

You will read stories about many different games in this unit. What would you like to learn about games? Write two questions on the lines. You may find the answers as you read.

_____

_____

_____

43

Lesson 5

GETTING READY TO READ

The first story you will read is "Street Games." What is your favorite street game? Why do you like to play this game?

What Do You Think You Will Learn?

Look at pages 45 through 48. Look at the pictures. What do you think the story will be about? Draw a line under the sentence that tells what you think.

I will learn about games kids play outdoors.

I will learn about games kids play in the house.

STREET GAMES

Children always find places outdoors to play games. Here are four games you can play.

Bottle Caps

Flick! Click! To play bottle caps, get chalk, four bottle caps, and four people.

Draw a gameboard on the sidewalk. Then line up four bottle caps in a row. Take turns "flicking" the caps with your thumb and third finger. Whoever flicks farthest goes first.

To win, you must flick into each box in 1, 2, 3 order. You can try to knock a player's cap out of a box. On his or her turn, that player has to get the cap back in the box to start again! It's all part of the fun!

This is the gameboard for bottle caps. Each bottle cap must go in order from box 1 to box 9.

These girls are jumping away from the ball. They are dodging the ball.

Dodgeball

Children ducking! Balls flying through the air! Dodge that ball!

Get about ten people together. Decide where you want to play. Use chalk to draw a big field. Then draw a line across the center of the field. Make two teams. Each team stands on one side of the line. To start, a player on one team throws a big ball at a player on the other team. The point is not to get hit by the ball!

Are you in the game? Then jump and leap. Get out of the way. Dodge the ball. If the ball hits you, you're out of the game. If you catch the ball, the player who threw it is out of the game! Now throw the ball. The first team to lose all its players loses the game.

Hit the Penny

Keep your eye on the penny. It looks easy! Try it and see what you think.

Play this street game with a friend. Put a penny on a crack in the sidewalk. Then take turns throwing a ball. Try to hit the penny or to flip it over.

Each time you hit the penny, you win one point. If you flip the penny, you get five points. If you move the penny without flipping it, you don't get any points. Whoever gets twenty points first wins the game.

The girl is trying to hit the penny. She aims the ball at the penny.

Hopscotch

Hopscotch is a great street game. It's easy to play. All you need are a stone, chalk, and some friends.

First, draw a hopscotch board. Number the boxes. Take turns. Throw a stone into box 1. Hop over box 1 and into boxes 2 and 3. Then hop to the last box, turn around, and hop back.

Then go again. Throw your stone into box 2. Hop around again. Keep going. When you get to the last box, you win!

Don't step on a line or jump out of a box. If you do, you'll lose a turn!

Hopscotch is fun! So are bottle caps, dodgeball, and hit the penny! These games can be played anywhere there's a street or a sidewalk.

So get some friends together. Flick and dodge. Hit the penny and hop. Enjoy!

▲ Children drew this hopscotch board on the sidewalk.

48

Lesson 5

After Reading

What Did You Learn?

You have read "Street Games" for the first time. What did you think you would find out? Look on page 44 to help you remember. Which street game would you like to learn? Tell about it. Write on the lines below. You can look back at the story to help you.

_____

_____

_____

Check Your Understanding

Use one of the words in the box to finish each sentence.

| penny | caps | hopscotch | dodgeball |

1. In _____ a player tries not to get hit by the ball.

2. Players use a ball to flip or hit a _____ in this street game.

3. Players have to throw a stone and hop to play _____.

4. Players flick bottle _____ to try to win this game.

49

Lesson 5

Word Analysis — Long Vowels

Letter patterns can help you read a word. Look at the pattern of consonants and vowels in the word **team**.

consonant → **t** **e** **a** **m** ← consonant
         vowel ↗   ↖ vowel

Sometimes words with this letter pattern have the long sound of the first vowel. Say the word **team** out loud. Listen for the **long e** sound.

Say each picture name. Listen for the vowel sound. Circle the word that names the picture. Write the name if the letters fit the **CVVC** pattern.

1. nail / net _____

2. cat / coat _____

3. gain / gas _____

4. feet / bed _____

5. rode / toad _____

6. mail / sell _____

7. dark / desk _____

8. jet / jeans _____

50

Lesson 5

Vocabulary — Multiple Meanings

Some words have more than one meaning. The word foot can mean "part of the body" or "12 inches." Look at other words in the sentence. Then you can tell what the word means. Look at this sentence.

Some players like to hop on one foot.

In this sentence, foot means "part of the body." You use your foot to hop.

Read the sentences below. Darken the circle that tells the meaning of each word in dark print.

1. The ball will **fly** through the air.
   - Ⓐ small insect
   - Ⓑ move quickly
   - Ⓒ escape

2. You **duck** your head when the ball is coming!
   - Ⓐ dodge
   - Ⓑ animal
   - Ⓒ run away

3. Line up all the bottle caps in a neat **row**.
   - Ⓐ paddle
   - Ⓑ line
   - Ⓒ noise

4. Hit the penny with a **ball**.
   - Ⓐ round object
   - Ⓑ dance
   - Ⓒ good time

Words That Were New to You

Choose words from the story that were new to you. Use a dictionary to check the meanings. Add the words and their meanings to your word list on page 127.

51

Lesson 5

REREADING

Main Idea

The main idea is the most important idea in a paragraph. Read this paragraph.

> Children like to play street games for many reasons. The games are easy to play. There are many kinds of street games. Best of all, street games are fun!

The first sentence tells the most important idea. Other sentences tell more about this idea.

Read the story again. Look for the main idea of these games. Then underline the sentence that tells the main idea.

1. Bottle caps

    Play bottle caps on a big board.

    Get your bottle cap into each box.

    "Flick" the bottle cap to play.

2. Dodgeball

    Try to catch the ball.

    Play dodgeball on a big field.

    Don't get hit with the ball.

3. Hit the Penny

    Place the penny on a sidewalk crack.

    Hit or flip a penny with a ball.

    Take turns throwing the ball.

Lesson 5

Sequence

You have to play games in a certain order. Put these sentences in the correct order. Write 1, 2, or 3 on the lines before each sentence to tell how to play dodgeball.

_____ Throw the ball at a player on the other team.

_____ Draw a large field with a line down the middle.

_____ Make two teams, one on each side of the line.

Think and Write

You have read about different street games. Choose one activity about street games.

1. Suppose you and your friends decided to make up a new street game. What kind of game would it be? What would you need to play the game? Write about the game. Tell about the rules and how to play.

2. Find out about street games children played 100 years ago in big cities. Use the encyclopedia or other books at the library. Write a short report.

3. Suppose you wanted to have a street games Olympics. What games would you play? How would players get on the teams? Write about how you would hold the games.

Lesson 6

GETTING READY TO READ

Children all over the world like to play games. The next story you will read is "Games Around the World." What games do you like to play? Why do you like to play them?

What Do You Think You Will Learn?

Look at pages 55 through 58. Look at the pictures. What do you think the story will be about? Draw a line under the sentence that tells what you think.

I will learn about games children play in other countries.

I will learn what children do in school.

54

GAMES AROUND THE WORLD

All over the world, children play different games. Some of the games may be like games you have played. Others may be new and different.

Children in China like to play a game with their kites. They have kite fights. Two or three children can play this game together.

The children make their kite strings rough, not smooth. Then they find ways to cross the strings of their kites. The kite strings rub together in the air. One kite string cuts another string. The kite falls to the ground. The children have to fix the kite. Soon it is flying again.

Kites have many shapes. This kite is in the shape of a bird.

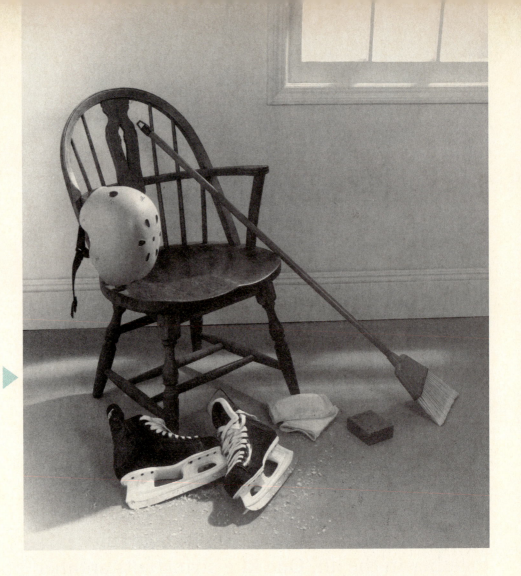

This is what children use to play broom hockey.

Imagine a playing field made on ice. A field of ice is used to play a game called broom hockey. Children in Canada like to play this game.

In broom hockey, there are two teams. Six players are on each team. Players use old brooms for sticks. They paint a piece of wood a bright color. Then the players try to hit the wood with their brooms.

There is a circle at each end of the playing field. Each circle belongs to a different team. Players try to hit the wood into the circle of the other team. Do you know a game that is like broom hockey?

Do you ever play checkers? Children in Africa play a game like checkers. It is called yote (YOH tee).

Yote is played on the ground. There are holes in the ground. There are five rows. Each row has six holes.

Two children play. They take turns putting pebbles in the holes. They put pebbles all over the board. The children don't want to put their pebbles in holes next to each other. If they do, the other player can jump over that hole and take the pebble.

The winner is the player who gets the most pebbles.

These African children are playing yote.

The boy is trying to hit the piñata. What do you think is inside?

These people are at a party in Mexico. They are playing a special game with a paper star. The paper star is called a piñata. The piñata is filled with candy and small toys.

One player's eyes are covered with a piece of cloth. Then that player tries to hit the piñata with a stick. The piñata is hard to find! Other players tell the child where to turn. A player has three chances to hit the piñata. Then someone else has a turn. Finally someone hits the piñata! It breaks open. Candy and toys drop to the ground. All the children run to pick them up!

You have read about different games. Have you ever played any of them? Which one would you like to play?

Lesson 6

AFTER READING

What Did You Learn?

You have read "Games Around the World" for the first time. What did you think you would find out? Look on page 54 to help you remember. Did you learn anything new? Tell about it. Write on the lines below. You can look back at the story to help you.

_____
_____
_____
_____

Check Your Understanding

Darken the circle next to the word that best completes each sentence.

1. In China, children play a game with _____.
   Ⓐ cars Ⓑ balloons Ⓒ kites

2. In Canada, children play a game on the ice with _____.
   Ⓐ boats Ⓑ brooms Ⓒ kites

3. Yote is a game that children play with _____.
   Ⓐ strings Ⓑ pebbles Ⓒ cloth

4. A piñata is filled with _____.
   Ⓐ sticks Ⓑ cans Ⓒ toys

59

Lesson 6

Word Analysis — Long Vowels

Letter patterns can help you read a word. Look at the pattern of consonants and vowels in the word **kite**.

consonant → **k i t e** ← silent e
vowel ↗ ↖ consonant

Sometimes words with this letter pattern have the long sound of the first vowel. Say the word **kite** out loud. Listen for the **long i** sound.

Look at these pictures. Say each picture name. Listen for the vowel sound. Write the missing letters that fit the **CVC + silent e** pattern.

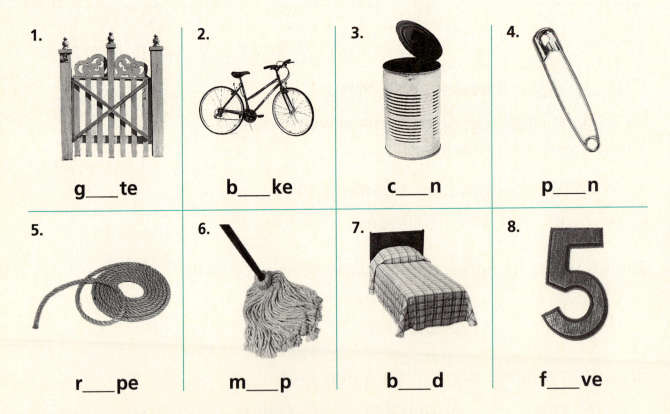

1. g___te
2. b___ke
3. c___n
4. p___n
5. r___pe
6. m___p
7. b___d
8. f___ve

Look back at the story. Find two words that have the **CVC + silent e** pattern. Write the words.

_____   _____

60

Lesson 6

Vocabulary — Antonyms

Antonyms are words that have opposite meanings. The words hot and cold are antonyms. You can use antonyms to help you find the meaning of a new word. Read this sentence.

> The children make their kite strings rough, not smooth.

The word not is a clue that smooth is the opposite of rough. So, rough means "not smooth."

Read these sentences. Write the antonym for the word in dark print.

1. We were **glad** that our team won the game.

   The other team was _____.

   happy   sad

2. A piñata cannot hold **huge** toys. Only

   _____ toys can fit inside it.

   tiny   big

3. The ground was too **wet** to play yote. We had to wait until the ground was

   _____.

   dry   clean

Words That Were New to You

Choose words from the story that were new to you. Use a dictionary to check the meanings. Add the words and their meanings to your word list on page 127.

61

Lesson 6

REREADING

Compare and Contrast

Sometimes two things are alike. Sometimes two things are different.

Read these sentences about how kites and piñatas are alike and different.

1. Kites and piñatas are alike. They are both made of paper.

2. Kites and piñatas are different. Kites can fly. Piñatas cannot fly.

A diagram can show how kites and piñatas are alike and different.

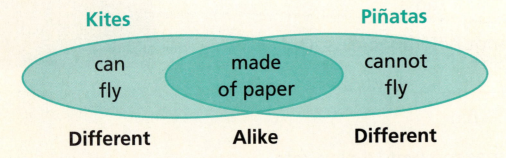

Reread "Games Around the World." Then finish this alike and different diagram.

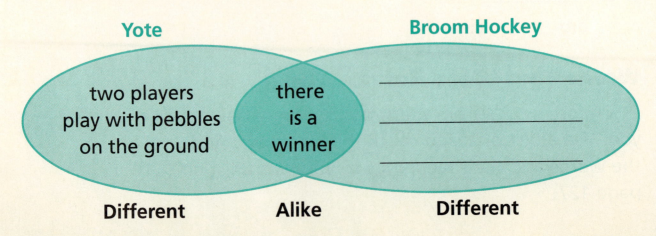

Lesson 6

Use the story and the diagram to answer these questions.

1. How are yote and broom hockey alike?

   _____

2. How are yote and broom hockey different?

   _____

Main Idea

Underline the sentence that tells the main idea of "Games Around the World."

1. Children play broom hockey in Canada.

2. Children play different games in different countries.

3. Children play with kites in China.

You have read about different games all over the world. Choose one activity about games.

1. Plan how you would make a kite. Draw a picture of it. Then write about your kite.

2. Write a letter to a friend. Tell about the game you liked best.

3. Find a fact about a country in this story. Use a book in your school library to help you.

Lesson 7

GETTING READY TO READ

The story that you are going to read is "The Jump Rope Kids." You might not believe what they can do!

What Do You Think You Will Learn?

Look at pages 65 through 68. Look at the pictures. What do you think the story will be about? Draw a line under the sentence that tells what you think.

I will learn about kids who play hopscotch.

I will learn about kids who jump rope.

64

The JUMP ROPE Kids

Have you ever jumped rope? How many times can you jump in a minute? Take a guess. One boy can jump 150 times in one minute! Another kid can do back flips. Some kids even dance and jump at the same time.

The kids are all part of a team. The team is called the Happy Hoppers. They go to Whittier Elementary School. The school is in Dayton, Ohio.

The Hoppers use "pogo balls" to help them take off.

65

The Happy Hoppers learned their jump rope tricks from Coach Woody Pumphrey. He came up with a good idea. The coach wanted the kids to have something to do after school. He had only one rule for the team. Everyone had to get good grades.

There are about 50 kids on the team. They are between the ages of 7 and 13. All of them jump rope because it's fun. They like to learn new tricks.

Coach Pumphrey has Hoppers jumping through hoops!

The kids also work hard. Jump rope tricks take a lot of practice. Hoppers work out for hours at a time. They repeat their hard jumps again and again. They practice jumping in pairs. They practice new dances. They practice jumping fast!

The long hours of practice really pay off. The Hoppers can twist and turn their way through double Dutch back flips. One Hopper named Elizabeth Ankeny wears roller skates when she jumps. Some of the kids can jump rope while they are on pogo balls.

Remember the kid who jumped 150 times in a minute? His name is Julian Addison. And, when it comes to jumping rope, Julian is one of the best. He set a new rope skipping record for kids his age.

One of these Hoppers is head over heels about jumping.

(Do not try this on your own.)

67

The Happy Hoppers are always busy. They give shows all over Ohio. They also enter many contests. They jump rope against kids from other states and countries.

Can you count how many Hoppers are in this picture?

Hoppers win prizes for their special jumps and spins. But for the Hoppers, working together as a team is even better than winning prizes. They like to practice! They really like to try out new jump rope tricks. It's hard work, but it sure is fun!

Lesson 7

AFTER READING

What Did You Learn?

You have read "The Jump Rope Kids" for the first time. What did you think you would find out? Look on page 64 to help you remember. What did you learn that surprised you? Tell about it. Write on the lines below. You can look back at the story to help you.

_____

_____

_____

Check Your Understanding

Use one of the words in the box to finish each sentence.

practice	contests	grades	coach

1. The Happy Hoppers learned their jump rope tricks from their _____.

2. Happy Hoppers have to get good _____ to be on the team.

3. It takes a lot of _____ to be good at jump rope.

4. The Happy Hoppers enter many _____.

69

Lesson 7

Word Analysis — Consonant Blends

Say each picture name. Listen to the beginning sound of each word. You can hear the sound that both beginning letters stand for. You can hear a **blend** of two sounds.

| **st**ove | **sk**ate | **sp**ider | **tw**ins |

Read these sentences about the story. Find the word in each sentence that begins with a blend of two sounds. Write each word on the line.

1. Hoppers can twist and turn. _____

2. He set a new rope skipping record. _____

3. The Hoppers enter contests in many states. _____

4. Hoppers can do special jumps. _____

Say each picture name. Circle the word that names the picture.

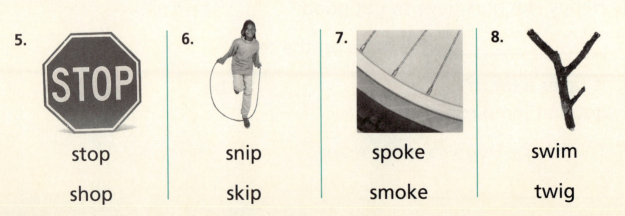

5. stop / shop

6. snip / skip

7. spoke / smoke

8. swim / twig

70

Lesson 7

Vocabulary — Context Clues

When you read, you may not know a word. Look at other words in the sentence. They may help you figure out the meaning of the new word. Read this sentence.

>Everyone yells and cheers happily when the Hoppers come out to jump rope.

You may not know what cheers means. Read the other words in the sentence. You can figure out that cheers probably means "to yell happily."

Read these sentences. Circle the meaning of the word in dark print. Use the words in the sentence to help you.

1. They **repeat** their hard jumps again and again.

    do something over and over

    do something fun

2. They can **twist** and turn their way through double Dutch back flips.

    break   bend

3. The Hoppers enter special jump rope **contests** against other teams.

    games   sticks

Words That Were New to You

Choose words from the story that were new to you. Use a dictionary to check the meanings. Add the words and their meanings to your word list on page 127.

71

Lesson 7

Rereading

Drawing Conclusions

Writers don't always tell readers everything. Sometimes you have to figure it out. You can use clues in the story to help. When you use clues to figure out what is happening, you are **drawing conclusions**. Read these sentences.

> Sabrina remembers Whittier Elementary. She became a Happy Hopper there. Sabrina learned many jump rope tricks when she was a Happy Hopper.

You know that only Whittier students can join the Happy Hoppers. Sabrina is remembering Whittier. This clue tells you that she does not go there anymore. You can draw a conclusion that Sabrina isn't a Happy Hopper anymore.

Reread the story. Darken the circle next to the words that best complete each sentence.

1. All the kids on the Happy Hoppers
   - Ⓐ like math.
   - Ⓑ get good grades.
   - Ⓒ eat apples.

2. The Happy Hoppers are all
   - Ⓐ good roller skaters.
   - Ⓑ hard workers.
   - Ⓒ good swimmers.

3. The Happy Hoppers
   - Ⓐ take trips.
   - Ⓑ only jump at Whittier Elementary.
   - Ⓒ stay in Dayton.

Lesson 7

Compare and Contrast

Another jumping team is the Jumping Jacks. The diagram below tells you about the Jumping Jacks. Finish the diagram by telling how the Happy Hoppers are different.

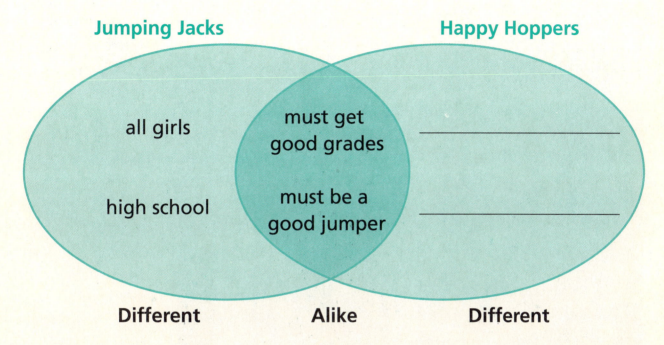

You have read about the Happy Hoppers. Choose one activity to complete.

1. Make up a jump rope trick of your own. Tell about it. Draw a picture of it.

2. Plan a team for your friends. Write about it.

3. Suppose the Happy Hoppers came to your town. Make a poster telling why people should see them.

73

Lesson 8

GETTING READY TO READ

Has an older person ever told you about a game he or she played a long time ago? The story you are about to read is "A New Old Game." What games from long ago do you know about?

What Do You Think You Will Learn?

Look at pages 75 through 78. Look at the pictures. Think about the story name. What do you think the story will be about? Draw a line under the sentence that tells what you think.

I will learn about a trip to a new place.

I will learn about a game from long ago.

74

A New Old Game

It was a clear, bright day. Tony, Eric, and Annie walked quickly home from school. They wanted to have time to play.

Tony held out a big ball. "Let's go to the field," he said. "We'll play kickball!"

"That's great!" Annie said. "Let's go!"

"We always play kickball. I'm tired of that game," Eric yelled.

He headed home alone.

When Eric got home, he went to see his grandfather. Grandfather was painting a clay pot. Behind him were other beautiful pots. Eric sat down. He liked to watch his grandfather paint. Each pot told a story from long ago. Often his grandfather told him the story as he painted.

"Why aren't you playing with your friends?" his grandfather asked.

"I'm tired of kickball," Eric said. "I want to play a new game."

Grandfather carefully put the pot on the floor.

"I know a different game," Grandfather said. "My grandfather played it a long time ago."

"Long ago our people played this game with big hoops and long sticks. They played it after a buffalo hunt," Grandfather said.

"But I don't have any hoops. How could I play this game with my friends?" Eric asked.

"We can use something else," Grandfather said. "Let's go for a walk. We'll look around."

They walked to a big lot full of old tires. They picked out a fat tire and rolled it home. On the way, Grandfather told Eric about the game. "But, before you play," Grandfather said, "we have to paint the tire."

Eric and Grandfather painted pictures on the tire. On one side, they painted a red fox and a turtle. On the other side, they painted a bluebird and a rabbit.

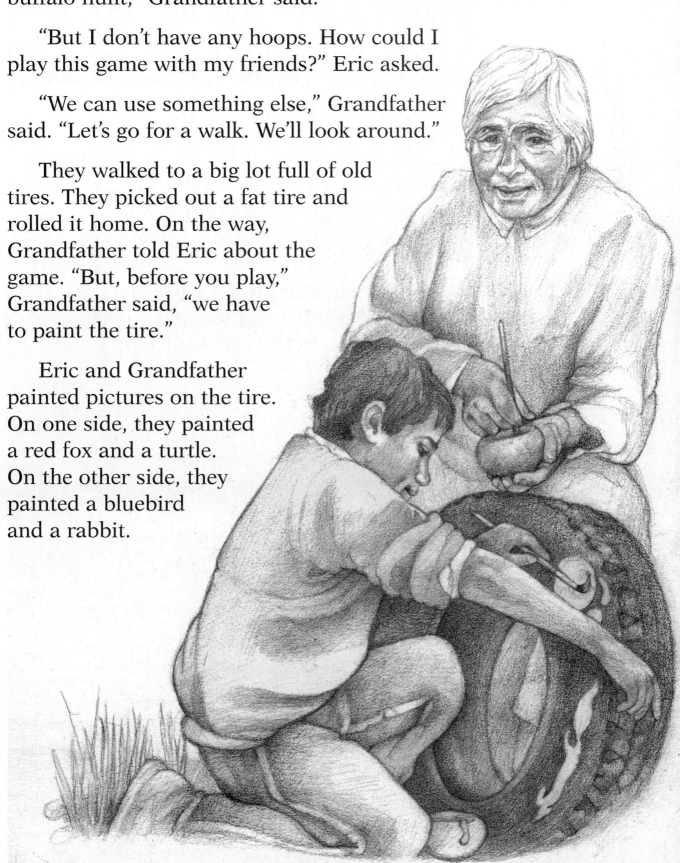

The next day, Eric rolled the tire outside. Tony and Annie were walking by.

"What's that for?" Annie said.

"It's a new old game my grandfather taught me," said Eric. "I roll the tire. You try to knock it down with a stick. But there's a trick! You have to call out the name of one of the pictures on the tire before it falls," Eric said. "If the tire lands on the picture, you win ten points. The first person to get to fifty points wins!"

Soon everyone was playing!

Eric's grandfather watched through the window. He thought of his own grandfather. He smiled.

Lesson 8

AFTER READING

What Did You Learn?

You have read "A New Old Game" for the first time. What did you think it would be about? Look on page 74 to help you remember. What did you find out that was new? Tell about it. Write on the lines below.

_____

_____

_____

Check Your Understanding

Darken the circle next to the word that best completes each sentence.

1. Eric is tired of playing _____ with his friends.
   Ⓐ baseball   Ⓑ kickball   Ⓒ dodgeball

2. Eric's grandfather teaches him a _____ his people played.
   Ⓐ song   Ⓑ poem   Ⓒ game

3. People played the game after a _____ hunt.
   Ⓐ fox   Ⓑ buffalo   Ⓒ rabbit

4. To play the game, first you have to paint _____ on a tire.
   Ⓐ numbers   Ⓑ stories   Ⓒ pictures

79

Lesson 8

Word Analysis — Consonant Blends

Say each picture name. Listen to the beginning sound of each word. You can hear the sound that both beginning letters stand for. You can hear a **blend** of two sounds.

plant   **cl**ock   **gr**apes   **tr**ee

Read these sentences about the story. Find the word in each sentence that begins with a blend of two sounds. Write each word on the line.

1. It was a clear day. _____

2. Eric wanted to play a new game. _____

3. His grandfather knew a different game. _____

Say each picture name. Circle the word that names the picture.

4. globe / robe

5. head / bread

6. dress / mess

7. grass / glass

80

Lesson 8

Vocabulary — Inflectional Endings

A verb is an action word. It tells what a person, place, or thing does. When the action is happening now, add the ending -s or -es to a verb. When the action happened in the past, add the ending -ed. Read these sentences.

1. Eric plays the game with his friends now.

2. Eric played the game with his friends before.

In sentence 1, -s is added to play. Plays tells what Eric is doing now. In sentence 2, -ed is added to play. Played tells what Eric did in the past.

Read these sentences. Circle the word that completes each sentence.

1. Grandfather _____ how to play the game long ago.

    learns   learned

2. Yesterday, Eric _____ Tony how to play.

    shows   showed

3. Now, Tony _____ he had his own painted tire.

    wishes   wished

Words That Were New to You

Choose words from the story that were new to you. Use a dictionary to check the meanings. Add the words and their meanings to your word list on page 127.

81

Lesson 8

Rereading

Dialogue

In a story, people talk to each other. The words people say are called **dialogue**. The words have special marks around them. The special marks are called **quotation marks**. The marks look like this " ". Read these sentences.

"I'm tired of kickball," Eric said. "I want to play a new game."

The sentences *"I'm tired of kickball. I want to play a new game"* are dialogue. These are the words that Eric said. These words are in quotation marks.

Read the story again. Look for places where people are talking. Look for clues that tell who is talking.

Read the dialogue below. Look back at page 75. Find the dialogue. Write who said the words.

1. "Let's go to the field. We'll play kickball!"

   _____

2. "That's great! Let's go."

   _____

3. "We always play kickball. I'm tired of that game."

   _____

82

Lesson 8

Drawing Conclusions

Circle the sentence that tells the conclusion you can draw after reading "A New Old Game." Use clues from the story to help you.

1. Eric had many pets.

2. Eric and his grandfather were good friends.

3. Eric liked to play kickball.

You have read about the game that Eric showed his friends. Use what you have learned to complete one of these activities.

1. Think about the game that Eric and his friends played with the tire. Imagine there's a Name That Game contest. Think of a name. Tell why it's a good name for the game.

2. If you played Eric's game, what pictures would you paint on the tire? Make a drawing of what you would use. Tell why you chose those pictures.

3. Think about how Native Americans played the game long ago. They used hoops. They played it after a buffalo hunt. Draw a picture of how the Native Americans might have played. Then write a few sentences about your picture.

83

UNIT

3 THE SKY ABOVE US

What is in the sky?

There is so much to see in the sky above us. During the day the sun shines and warms us. But after the sun sets, the sky becomes dark. There are many different stars in the night sky. Some are close to Earth. Others are very far away. Sometimes a star will even shoot across the sky.

Every day we learn more about the moon and the stars.

84

What Do You Already Know?

Look at these pictures. What do they make you think of? Write three words for each picture.

_____   _____

_____   _____

_____   _____

What Do You Want to Find Out?

You will read stories about the sky and some of the things in it. What do you want to find out about the sky above us? Write two questions on the lines. You may find the answers as you read.

_____

_____

_____

_____

_____

_____

85

Lesson 9

GETTING READY TO READ

The first story you will read is "All About Stars." What do you already know about stars? What would you like to find out?

What Do You Think You Will Learn?

Look at pages 87 through 90. Look at the pictures. What do you think you will learn in this story? Draw a line under the sentence that tells what you think.

I will learn about the moon.

I will learn about the stars in the sky.

ALL ABOUT STARS

Look up at the sky on a clear night. What do you see? The stars shine all around you. They look like dots of white chalk on black paper.

Stars are really great balls of hot, shining gas. Stars give out heat and light. The stars that look the brightest are often the ones that are closest to Earth.

The stars shine in the night sky.

Stars are always in the sky. You can't see them in the daytime. They are hidden by the light from the sun. But when the sun sets, the sky gets dark. Then you can see the stars shining in the night sky.

87

Astronomers are people who study stars. They know that stars are different sizes. The biggest stars are called supergiants. There are giants and medium-size stars. There are small stars called dwarf stars. The smallest stars are called neutron stars.

Stars are also different colors. The color of a star tells how hot the star is. The hottest stars are blue. There are white stars and yellow stars. The coolest stars are red. Our sun is a yellow dwarf star.

Some giant stars are blue. They are very hot. Other giant stars are red. They are much cooler.

The Life of a Star

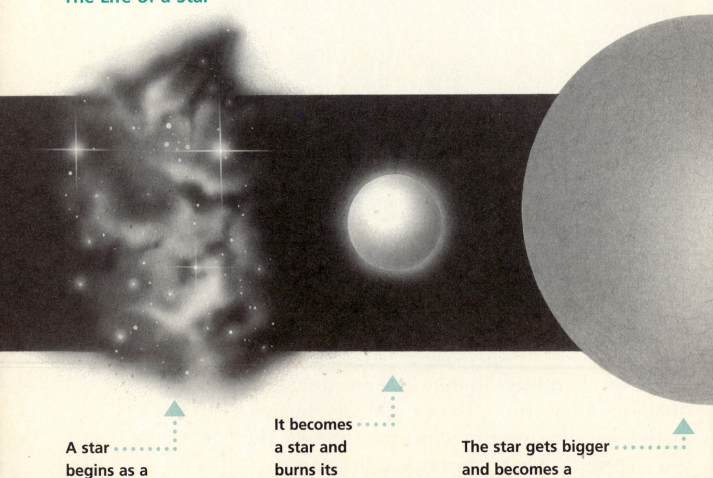

A star begins as a gas cloud.

It becomes a star and burns its gas.

The star gets bigger and becomes a supergiant.

88

A star begins as a large cloud of gas and dust. Over a very long time, the cloud then forms into the shape of a ball. It pulls more dust into the ball. The center of the ball gets very hot. Finally it is so hot that the outside of the ball begins to glow. The heat makes it shine. It is a star!

A star can live for millions of years. Then it begins to change. The inside gets hotter while the outside gets cooler. This makes the star get bigger and bigger. Sometimes a star gets so big that it blows up! Little pieces of the star are left. These little pieces can become tiny neutron stars.

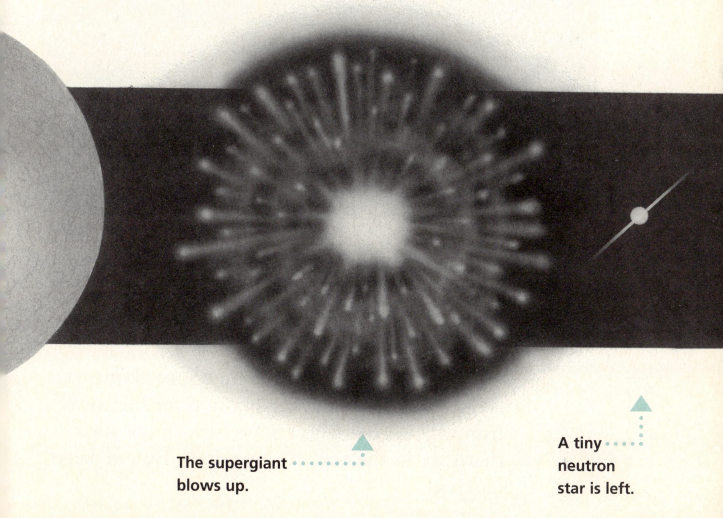

The supergiant blows up.

A tiny neutron star is left.

The sun is really a star. It is the most important star for the people on Earth. We need sunlight. Without the sun, Earth would be dark and cold. Nothing could live here.

The sun seems much bigger than other stars. It looks that way because it is closer to Earth. The sun is much larger than the Earth. But it is much smaller than many other stars.

This group of stars looks like a big soup spoon. It is called the Big Dipper.

Groups of stars can look like pictures in the sky. People have seen lions and bears and dogs made by stars in the sky. Have you ever seen any of these patterns?

Astronomers keep learning more about stars. They find stars farther and farther away from the Earth. Who knows how many stars there are in the sky? No one does. But we keep looking!

90

Lesson 9

AFTER READING

What Did You Learn?

You have read "All About Stars" for the first time. What did you think you would learn? Look on page 86 to help you remember. What did you learn that surprised you? Tell about it. Write on the lines below. You can look back at the story to help you.

_____

_____

_____

Check Your Understanding

Darken the circle next to the word that best completes each sentence.

1. Stars are balls of hot, shining _____.
   - Ⓐ clouds
   - Ⓑ gas
   - Ⓒ suns

2. Stars that are closer to the Earth look _____.
   - Ⓐ brighter
   - Ⓑ smaller
   - Ⓒ redder

3. The _____ is the most important star for people on Earth.
   - Ⓐ supergiant
   - Ⓑ Big Dipper
   - Ⓒ sun

4. Blue stars are _____ than other stars.
   - Ⓐ hotter
   - Ⓑ cooler
   - Ⓒ smaller

Lesson 9

Word Analysis — Consonant Digraphs (initial ch and wh)

Words that begin with **ch** have the same beginning sound that you hear in the word *chair*.

Words that begin with **wh** have the same beginning sound that you hear in the word *whale*.

Read this sentence from the story. Find the words in the sentence that have the same beginning sounds you hear at the beginning of *chair* and *whale*. Write the words on the lines.

1. They look like dots of white chalk on black paper.

_____   _____

Say each picture name. Listen for the beginning sound. Circle the word that names the picture.

2.	3.	4.	5.
wheel	chick	trip	geese
steel	kick	whip	cheese

Lesson 9

Vocabulary — Compound Words

A compound word is made up of two smaller words. When you see a compound word, look at the two smaller words. These words may help you find the meaning of the larger word.

Look at this sentence from the story.

We need sunlight.

Sunlight is a compound word. It is made up of the smaller words sun and light. Sunlight means "the light of the sun."

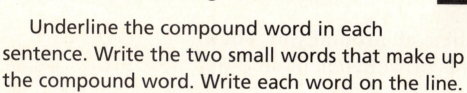

Underline the compound word in each sentence. Write the two small words that make up the compound word. Write each word on the line.

1. The sun is the only star we see in the daytime.

   _____   _____

2. Bright sunbeams shine on the ground.

   _____   _____

3. Starlight is really hot, shining gas.

   _____   _____

4. The biggest stars are called supergiants.

   _____   _____

Words That Were New to You

Choose words from the story that were new to you. Use a dictionary to check the meanings. Add the words and their meanings to your word list on page 128.

93

Lesson 9

REREADING

Word Referents

A **noun** names a person, place, or thing. A **pronoun** is a word that stands for a noun. Here are some pronouns.

| it | they | them | he | she | we |

Read these sentences from the story.

> The stars shine all around you. They look like dots of white chalk on black paper.

The word **they** is a pronoun. **They** stands for the noun **stars**. Read these sentences. The words in dark print are pronouns. Circle the noun that each pronoun stands for.

1. Marie is an astronomer. **She** studies the stars.

2. Some stars are blue. **They** are very hot.

3. The sun is important. People need **it** to live.

Read the story again. Look for pronouns and the nouns that they stand for. Read page 90. Find a pronoun. Find the noun that the pronoun stands for. Write the sentences on the lines. Circle the noun. Underline the pronoun.

Lesson 9

Sequence

Things happen in order. Put these sentences about how stars begin in the right order. Write the numbers 1, 2, or 3 on the lines in front of each sentence. Use the story to help you.

_____ Over a very long time, the cloud then forms into the shape of a ball.

_____ A star begins as a large cloud of gas and dust.

_____ The center of the ball gets very hot. Finally, it is so hot that the outside of the ball glows.

Think about what you have learned. Then complete one of these activities about stars.

1. Some stars have names. Look up information about stars in an encyclopedia. Find out the name of the brightest star and the largest star. Write one fact about each star.

2. Make a poster about stars for a school science fair. Write a sentence about stars on your poster.

3. Go outside on a clear night. Look at the stars. Pretend the stars are a connect the dots drawing. Can you find stars to make a picture? Draw the picture to share. Give it a name.

4. Look at the night sky. Find a special star. Give it a name. Write two sentences about it.

95

Lesson 10

GETTING READY TO READ

Suppose you could travel to another time and place. Where would you want to go? What do you think you would see? How would you get there? And how would you get home again? The story you are going to read is called "Traveling Through Time." And that's what it's about!

What Do You Think You Will Learn?

Look at pages 97 through 100. What do you think you will learn in this story? Draw a line under the sentence that tells what you think.

I will learn about José and Beth's classroom.

I will learn about José and Beth's class trip.

96

Traveling Through Time

The class trip was finally happening. The children were in the science museum. They were going to see the dinosaur models. Beth and José were very excited. Beth told José that she was too excited to sleep the night before. José said he didn't sleep either.

"Look," Beth said. "There's the room where they have the star show."

"We won't have time to go there today," the teacher said.

"But that's the best part," Beth cried. She looked at José. "We've got to get in there somehow," she said. José nodded.

The rest of the class went on ahead to the dinosaur room. José and Beth stayed behind. Then they turned and ran into the star room. The room was dark. A make-believe sky was filled with stars. A man was talking to a room full of people. Beth and José tiptoed to a seat.

"Look!" José yelled. "See that star. It's getting bigger! It's blowing apart!"

Clouds of white dust filled the room.

"This isn't make-believe!" Beth cried. "It's real. That star just died. And it left a black hole in the sky."

Just then there was a big whooshing sound. Beth and José were lifted off the ground. They were pulled into the black hole.

José and Beth landed with a thud. They were on the ground near a wide river.

"What happened?" Beth cried.

"Never mind what happened," José answered. "What's that?"

He pointed to the sky. A huge animal glided in the air. It didn't move its wings.

"I'm not sure," Beth said. "I'm more worried about what's over there. Look."

A giant dinosaur moved quickly across the ground. "Look at those big teeth," José cried. "That one eats meat!"

Just then another giant dinosaur got out of the water. It walked very slowly to a tall tree. It began to eat the shiny leaves at the top.

"That one has small teeth," Beth said. "It just eats leaves."

"How did we get here?" José cried. "How do we get back?"

"That black hole was like a time tunnel," Beth said. "That's how we got here."

"Look out!" José yelled.

A giant rock was falling to Earth. When it hit, the ground shook. There was a bright light!

José and Beth heard a man's voice say, "We think dinosaurs were killed after a giant rock fell from the sky."

Beth and José rubbed their eyes. They were in the star room. The lights were on.

"We fell asleep," Beth said. "And I had the strangest dream."

"Me, too," José answered. "Let's find the class. I think they're in the dinosaur room."

"Something makes me think I've seen the dinosaurs already," Beth smiled.

Lesson 10

AFTER READING

What Did You Learn?

You have read "Traveling Through Time" for the first time. What did you think you would learn? Look on page 96 to help you remember. What did you learn that was new? Tell about it. Write on the lines below. You can look back at the story to help you.

_____

_____

_____

Check Your Understanding

Use one of the words in the box to finish each sentence.

| dream | star | dinosaur | sleep |

1. Beth and José didn't _____ on the night before their class trip to the museum.

2. The place Beth and José wanted to see the most was the _____ room.

3. The rest of the class went to see the _____ room.

4. José and Beth's time travel was really a _____.

101

Lesson 10

Word Analysis — Consonant Digraphs (initial sh and th)

Words that begin with **sh** have the same beginning sound that you hear in the word **shoe**.

Words that begin with **th** have the same beginning sound that you hear in the words **thumb** or **them**.

Read these sentences from the story. Circle the words that have the same beginning sounds you hear in **shoe** and in **thumb**.

1. It began to eat the shiny leaves at the top.

2. We think dinosaurs were killed after a giant rock fell from the sky.

Say each picture name. Listen for the beginning sound. Circle the word that names the picture.

3.

bell

shell

4.

corn

thorn

5.

thirteen

twenty

6.

ship

skip

102

Lesson 10

Vocabulary — Contractions

Sometimes two words are put together to make a shorter word. The shorter word is called a **contraction**. Look at these words.

| do not → don't |
| she will → she'll |

The words *do* and *not* were put together to make *don't*. In the word *don't*, an **apostrophe** takes the place of the letter *o*. An apostrophe looks like this **'**. Sometimes the apostrophe takes the place of more than one letter. The contraction *she'll* stands for *she will*. The apostrophe takes the place of the letters *wi*.

Read these sentences. Darken the circle next to the two words that the contraction stands for.

1. "**We've** got to get in there somehow," she said.
   - Ⓐ We have
   - Ⓑ We will
   - Ⓒ We should

2. "This **isn't** make-believe!" Beth cried.
   - Ⓐ is not
   - Ⓑ does not
   - Ⓒ can not

3. "**I'm** not sure," Beth said.
   - Ⓐ I had
   - Ⓑ I will
   - Ⓒ I am

Words That Were New to You

Choose words from the story that were new to you. Use a dictionary to check the meanings. Add the words and their meanings to your word list on page 128.

Lesson 10

REREADING

Reality and Fantasy

Some stories are about things that could happen in real life. These stories are **real**. Other stories are about things that could not happen in real life. These stories are **make-believe**.

Sometimes real and make-believe things can happen in the same story. Read these sentences about "Traveling Through Time."

1. Beth and José visited the science museum.

2. Beth and José fell through a black hole to the time of the dinosaurs.

Sentence 1 is about people doing real things. Sentence 2 is about people doing things that could not really happen.

Read "Traveling Through Time" again. Then read the sentences below. On the line before each sentence, write **R** if it is real. Write **M** if it is make-believe.

_____ 1. José and Beth's class went to the science museum.

_____ 2. The class went to see the dinosaur room.

_____ 3. Beth and José went to the time of the dinosaurs.

_____ 4. Beth and José saw a giant rock hit Earth.

_____ 5. Beth and José fell asleep in the star room.

104

Lesson 10

Compare and Contrast

Use the diagram below to compare the two dinosaurs that José and Beth saw in the story. You can look back at the story to help you.

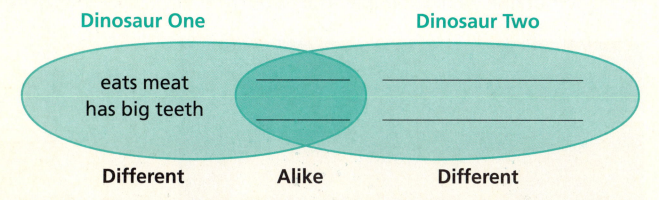

Dinosaur One — eats meat, has big teeth

Different | Alike | Different

Use your diagram to write a sentence telling how the dinosaurs are alike or different.

Think about José and Beth's travels back in time. Then complete one of these activities.

1. Suppose you could go back in time. What time would you go back to? Why? Write about your ideas.

2. Draw a picture of José and Beth falling through the black hole to the time of the dinosaurs. Write about your picture.

3. Suppose Beth and José had stayed in the time of the dinosaurs. What would have happened to them? Write your own story about it.

Lesson 11

GETTING READY TO READ

The next story you will read is "The Changing Moon." What do you already know about the moon? What else would you like to find out?

What Do You Think You Will Learn?

Look at pages 107 through 110. Look at the pictures and the headings on each page. What do you think you will learn about the moon from this story? Draw a line under the sentence that tells what you think.

I will learn why the moon changes shape.

I will learn about the man in the moon.

THE
Changing Moon

People on Earth have always had special feelings about the moon. They write poems about the moon. They look at the moon and make wishes. They study the moon.

The moon looks like a round ball hanging in the sky.

Why Does the Moon Shine?

The moon is easy to see in the black night sky. Most of the time it looks brighter than any star. But the moon does not give out light. It shines because it is getting light from the sun.

107

What Does the Moon Look Like?

The moon seems to have many shapes. There are times when you can't see it at all. Other times the moon looks like half a dish. Sometimes the moon looks like the top part of your fingernail. And, there are times when the moon looks like a round circle of light.

What Are the Phases of the Moon?

The moon is always moving. As it moves, its shape seems to change. Changes in the moon's shape have a special name. They are called phases of the moon.

Watch the moon every night for a month. It will seem to change shape. You will see the phases of the moon.

New Moon ···· Crescent Moon ···· Half Moon ···· Full Moon ····

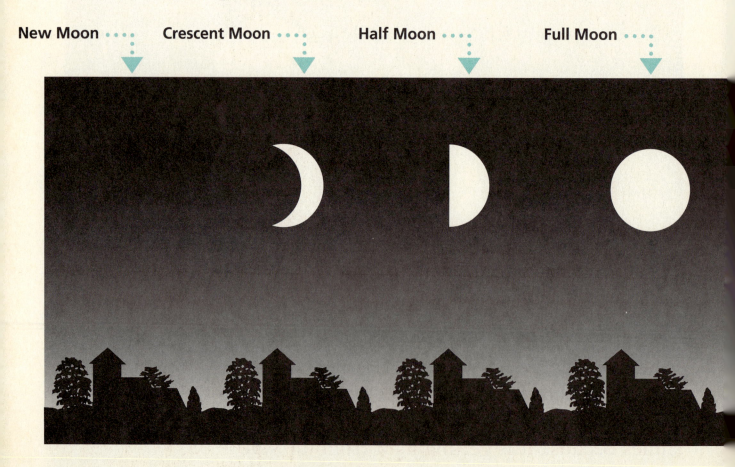

108

The new moon is the beginning of the moon's trip around Earth. The moon is between Earth and the sun. We can't see the moon at all. This first phase is called new moon.

The moon moves. We see what looks like part of a fingernail. This is called crescent moon. The moon keeps moving. It looks like half a moon. This next phase is called half moon.

Next the moon is full. It looks like a white dish. We call this phase full moon.

The moon does not stay full very long. It keeps moving around Earth. It becomes a half moon again. Finally, it is back to the beginning. Then it starts a new trip. It is a new moon again. We can't see it at all.

Half Moon   **Crescent Moon**   **New Moon**

These are the phases of the moon.

109

Why Does the Moon Change Shape?

The moon travels around Earth. This trip takes about one month. As the moon goes around Earth, the sun lights up different parts of the moon. We see only the parts that the sun lights up.

The sun lights up different parts of the moon.

110

Lesson 11

AFTER READING

What Did You Learn?

You have read "The Changing Moon" for the first time. What did you think you would learn? Look on page 106 to help you remember. Did you learn anything new? Tell about it. Write on the lines below. You can look back at the story to help you.

_____

_____

_____

Check Your Understanding

Darken the circle next to the word that best completes each sentence.

1. The moon travels around _____.

    Ⓐ Earth　　Ⓑ the sun　　Ⓒ the stars

2. The different shapes of the moon are called _____.

    Ⓐ new moons　Ⓑ phases　Ⓒ crescents

3. The light of the moon comes from the _____.

    Ⓐ stars　　Ⓑ moonlight　Ⓒ sun

4. The moon looks brighter than _____.

    Ⓐ the sun　　Ⓑ any star　　Ⓒ daylight

Lesson 11

Word Analysis — Consonant Digraphs (final sh and ck)

Words that end with **sh** have the same sound that you hear at the end of the word **brush**.

Words that end with **ck** have the same sound that you hear at the end of the word **sock**.

Read these sentences from the story. Circle the words that have the same ending sounds you hear in **brush** and in **sock**.

1. It looks like a white dish.

2. Finally, it is back to the beginning.

Say each picture name. Listen for the ending sound. Write the letters **sh** or **ck** to complete the picture name.

3.
fi____

4.
clo____

5.
chi____

6.
lo____

112

Lesson 11

Vocabulary — Multiple Meanings

Some words have more than one meaning. The word trip can mean "to travel" or "to fall." Look at this sentence from the story.

> This trip takes about one month.

You can tell the meaning of trip by looking at other words around it. The words about one month are clues. It can't take one month to fall. But it can take that long to travel someplace.

Read the sentences below. Circle the correct meaning of the word in dark print.

1. The moon does not give out **light**.

    not heavy   a bright shine

2. The moon's shape seems to **change**.

    money   become different

3. Sometimes we can only see **part** of the moon.

    one piece   a line in hair

Pick a word in dark print from the sentences above. Use the other meaning of that word in a sentence.

Words That Were New to You

Choose words from the story that were new to you. Use a dictionary to check the meanings. Add the words and their meanings to your word list on page 128.

113

Lesson 11

REREADING

Sequence

You have learned about the order of the phases of the moon. There is also an order to the way things happen in a story.

Read these sentences about "The Changing Moon."

> The first phase is called new moon.
> The next phase is called crescent moon.

These sentences are clues to **time order**. The word **first** helps us understand that this is where the moon begins its trip. The word **next** is a clue that things have already happened before. As you read, look for other clue words. They will help you keep track of time order.

Read "The Changing Moon" again. Look for the different phases the moon goes through from one new moon to the next. Then put these sentences in time order. Write 1, 2, 3, or 4 on the lines next to each sentence.

_____ After the new moon, we see a crescent moon.

_____ The new moon comes at the beginning of the moon's trip around the Earth.

_____ After the crescent moon, we see a half moon.

_____ Then we see a full moon.

114

Lesson 11

Reality and Fantasy

Read these sentences from "Traveling Through Time" and "The Changing Moon." Write R on the line if the sentence tells about something that could really happen. Write M on the line for make-believe.

_____ 1. Beth and José were lifted off the ground. They were pulled into the black hole.

_____ 2. The moon is always moving. As it moves, its shape seems to change.

_____ 3. The moon travels around Earth. The trip takes about one month.

Think and Write

Think about what you have learned. Then complete one of these activities.

1. Look at the moon in the night sky. Draw a picture of it. Then tell what the moon looks like to you.

2. Plan a trip to the moon. What would you take with you? What would you do there? Tell about it.

3. Make a moon calendar. Go outside and look at the moon each night. Draw a picture of the moon each time its shape looks very different. Tell how the shape changes.

115

Lesson 12

GETTING READY TO READ

The story you are about to read is "A Summer to Remember." Do you remember a summer that was special? What do you remember about it?

What Do You Think You Will Learn?

Look at pages 117 through 120. Look at the pictures. What do you think you will learn in this story? Draw a line under the sentence that tells what you think.

I will learn about fishing.

I will learn about summer in the country.

A Summer to Remember

Meg loved the city. She didn't think any place could be more fun. Then one day Meg was asked to spend a month with her cousin Pam. Pam lived in the country.

"The town is near the sea," Meg's mother said. "You'll love it there."

"What about my friend Jody?" she asked. "She'll be here without me!"

"You can always write to her. Tell her about the country," Mother said.

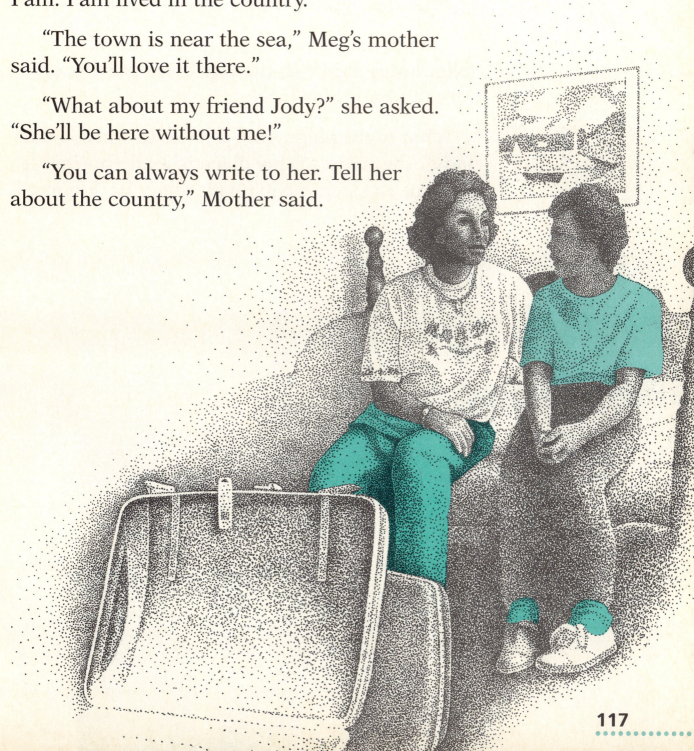

117

A week later Meg was walking on the beach with Pam. Pam was showing her around.

"That's the tallest place around here," Pam said. She pointed to the lighthouse. "Would you like to walk to the top one day?"

Meg didn't answer. She watched her feet sink into the hot sand. The lighthouse was boring to Meg. She didn't care about it.

"My apartment house in the city is much taller," Meg said. "In the city there are lots of very tall buildings."

That night Meg wrote a letter to Jody. "Dear Jody," she wrote. "This place is really boring. It puts me to sleep. I can't wait to get back home."

The next day, Meg walked to town with Pam and Uncle Ted. "Where's the bus?" Meg asked.

"We don't really need a bus," Pam answered. "We can walk everywhere."

"I bet we have a thousand buses in the city," Meg said. "I can ride anywhere."

"We may not have buses," Uncle Ted said. "But we do have something very special. Each summer we have a big party. It lasts all day. Everyone in town comes."

Meg didn't care. "How boring," she thought.

That night Meg wrote another letter to Jody. "This place is the biggest drag. Now I have to go to a silly party on Saturday."

Saturday was warm and sunny. Cooking smells filled the air. Everyone was having fun. Meg didn't even talk about the city.

At night the sky lit up with stars. "Look up," Pam said to Meg. "Can you find the stars that make the shape of a swan?"

Meg looked for a long time. "I can see it," she cried. "Over there are the wings."

Suddenly a white light raced across the sky again and again. Meg held her breath.

"Shooting stars!" someone yelled.

"You don't see them in the city," Meg said. "The sky is never this clear!"

That night Meg started another letter. "Dear Jody," she wrote. "You won't believe what I saw tonight! This place is great!"

Lesson 12

AFTER READING

What Did You Learn?

You have read "A Summer to Remember" for the first time. What did you think you would learn? Look on page 116 to help you remember. What did you find out that surprised you? Tell about it. Write on the lines below. You can look back at the story to help you.

_____

_____

_____

Check Your Understanding

Use one of the words in the box to complete each sentence.

country	lighthouse	city	fun

1. Meg loved the _____ more than any other place.

2. At first, Meg did not like living in the _____.

3. Meg thought the _____ was not very tall.

4. Pam showed Meg that the country can be _____.

121

Lesson 12

Word Analysis — Consonant Digraphs (final nk and ng)

Words that end with **nk** have the same sound that you hear at the end of the word **sink**.

Words that end with **ng** have the same sound that you hear at the end of the word **ring**.

Read these sentences from the story. Circle the words that have the same ending sounds you hear in **sink** or **ring**.

1. She didn't think any place could be more fun.

2. Cooking smells filled the air.

Say each picture name. Listen for the ending sound. Write the letters **nk** or **ng** to complete the picture name.

3. tru____   4. wi____   5. ta____   6. swi____

Choose one of the pictures above. Write a sentence using the picture name.

_____

122

Lesson 12

Vocabulary — Synonyms and Antonyms

Synonyms are words that have the same or almost the same meaning. **Antonyms** are words that have opposite meanings. Look at these sentences.

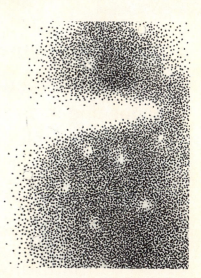

The stars looked tiny. They seemed very small.

The words **tiny** and **small** both tell about the size of the stars. They mean almost the same thing. They are synonyms. Read these sentences.

Meg thought the city was fun. It was not boring.

The word **not** is a clue. The words **fun** and **boring** are opposites. They are antonyms.

Read the sentences below. Look at the words in dark print. If they are opposites, write **A** for antonym. If they mean the same thing, write **S** for synonym.

_____ 1. Meg was **sad** to leave the city. She was not **happy** in the country.

_____ 2. The stars are **bright**. They are so **shiny**.

_____ 3. Saturday was **warm** and sunny. But the next day was **cold**.

Words That Were New to You

Choose words from the story that were new to you. Use a dictionary to check the meanings. Add the words and their meanings to your word list on page 128.

123

Lesson 12

Rereading

Drawing Conclusions

Sometimes you need to figure out what is happening in a story. Writers may not tell you what the people feel. You may have to guess. How do the people act? That is a clue. That will help you make your guess.

Read these sentences from the story.

> Saturday was warm and sunny. Cooking smells filled the air. Everyone was having fun. Meg didn't even talk about the city.

The writer does not tell you that Meg was having fun, too. You can tell by the way she acts. She doesn't talk about the city.

Reread the story. Think about what is happening. Darken the circle next to the sentence that gives a good guess about each page.

1. On page 117, a good guess would be

    Ⓐ Meg did not want to go to the country.

    Ⓑ Meg wanted to write to her friend.

    Ⓒ Meg was tired of living in the city.

2. On page 118, a good guess would be

    Ⓐ Pam wanted to visit the city.

    Ⓑ Meg missed her parents.

    Ⓒ Meg thought the city was better than the country.

124

Lesson 12

Dialogue

Read the sentences. Circle the name of the person who is talking.

1. "Tell her about the country," Mother said.

2. "That's the tallest place around here," Pam said.

3. "We may not have buses," Uncle Ted said.

4. "You don't see them in the city," Meg said.

Think and Write

Think about the story. Then choose one activity to complete.

1. Find out one fact about shooting stars. Use a book in your school library to help you.

2. Imagine you had seen a shooting star. How would you feel? Write about it.

3. Imagine you are Jody. Pick one of Meg's letters. Write Meg back.

4. Suppose Pam decided to visit Meg in the city. What do you think Pam and Meg might do together? Make up a plan for them.

Unit 1 — Animal Friends

MY WORD LIST

Unit 2 — Games Kids Play

MY WORD LIST

Unit 3 — The Sky Above Us

MY WORD LIST